JEALOUS GIRL?

Girls Dealing With Feelings

Other titles in this series:

Angry Girl?
Girls Dealing With Feelings
ISBN 978-1-62293-030-2

Feeling Unloved?
Girls Dealing With Feelings
ISBN 978-1-62293-050-0

Hassled Girl?
Girls Dealing With Feelings
ISBN 978-1-62293-035-7

Lonely Girl?
Girls Dealing With Feelings
ISBN 978-1-62293-055-5

Stressed-Out Girl?
Girls Dealing With Feelings
ISBN 978-1-62293-040-1

VAUGHAN PUBLIC LIBRARIES

J
155
.533
Sny

33288900636915

Jul 14, 2015

BC   Jealous girl? : girls dealing with feeli

WITHDRAWN

JEALOUS GIRL?

Girls Dealing With Feelings

Gail Snyder

JASMINE
HEALTH
Wellness • Diet • Cooking

Copyright © 2015 by Enslow Publishers, Inc.

Jasmine Health, an imprint of Enslow Publishers, Inc.

All rights reserved.

No part of this book may be reproduced by any means without the written permission of the publisher.

Library of Congress Cataloging-in-Publication Data

Snyder, Gail.
 [Girls' guide to jealousy]
Jealous girl? : girls dealing with feelings / Gail Snyder.
 pages cm. — (Girls dealing with feelings)
 "Originally published in 2009 as the author's A girls' guide to jealousy."
Includes bibliographical references and index.
 Summary: "Explores the emotion of jealousy in young women and the best ways to deal with it and the situations that cause it. Includes real-life examples, quotes, facts, tips, and quizzes"—Provided by publisher.
 ISBN 978-1-62293-045-6—ISBN 978-1-62293-046-3 (pbk)—ISBN 978-1-62293-047-0 (ePUB)—ISBN 978-1-62293-048-7 (PDF)—ISBN 978-1-62293-049-4 (PDF) 1. Jealousy. 2. Girls—Life skills guides. I. Title.
 BF575.J4S69 2014
 155.5'33—dc23

2013015768

Future editions:
Paperback ISBN: 978-1-62293-046-3
Single-User PDF ISBN: 978-1-62293-048-7

EPUB ISBN: 978-1-62293-047-0
Multi-User PDF ISBN: 978-1-62293-049-4

Printed in the United States of America
072014 HF Group, North Manchester, IN
10 9 8 7 6 5 4 3 2 1

To Our Readers: We have done our best to make sure all Internet addresses in this book were active and appropriate when we went to press. However, the author and the publisher have no control over and assume no liability for the material available on those Internet sites or on other Web sites they may link to. Any comments or suggestions can be sent by e-mail to comments@enslow.com or to the address below.

Jasmine Health
Box 398, 40 Industrial Road
Berkeley Heights, NJ 07922
USA
www.jasminehealth.com

Illustration Credits: Shutterstock.com: Christos Georghiou (clipboard graphic), p. 52; freesoulproduction (thumbtack graphic), pp. 8, 9, 12, 16, 29, 30, 34, 50, 53, 57; Jami Garrison, p. 3; NLshop (therapy graphic), pp. 22, 31, 36, 37, 39, 43, 45, 48, 54, 59, 61; Seamartini Graphics (atom graphic), pp. 15, 28; vectorgirl (lightbulb graphic), p. 10, ; zayats-and-zayats (quotation graphic), pp. 10, 11, 21, 27, 58.

Cover Photo: Jami Garrison/Shutterstock.com

This book was originally published in 2009 as *A Girls' Guide to Jealousy*.

CONTENTS

1. Jealousy and Envy 6
2. How You Feel About Yourself 14
3. Are You an Envious or Jealous Person? 19
4. Sibling Rivalry 26
5. Feeling Jealous of Friends 33
6. Jealousy in Dating 42
7. Irrational Jealousy 49
8. Overcoming Your Green-Eyed Monster 56

Find Out More 63
(Books, Internet Addresses, and Hotlines)

Index 64

CHAPTER ONE

Jealousy and Envy

Katie and Ashley had been close friends since first grade. But when they started middle school, Katie's behavior began to bother Ashley. The two girls shared several classes, and whenever the teacher handed back the graded tests, Katie would ask Ashley what she got. Ashley's grade was usually a few points higher than Katie's. After hearing that news, Katie would go into a funk. "That's so not fair," she would say. "Things come too easy for you."

Ashley could not understand why Katie was being so competitive with her. And she didn't like it. The next time the girls got a test back, she refused to show Katie her paper. But Katie was determined to learn whether she had done better than Ashley. She turned to the teacher and demanded that he tell her.

Envy is what you feel when someone has something you don't have but that you really want. In Katie's situation, she envied Ashley because of her friend's ability to do well at school. Envy differs from jealousy, although people often use the word *jealous* when they mean *envious*. Envy refers to the intense desire to possess something you don't have, while jealousy occurs when you fear losing something (such as attention or affection) that you already have. For example, if Katie thought that her boyfriend, Josh, was paying too much attention to Ashley, Katie's fear of losing him would make her jealous of her friend. This book discusses the often painful emotions of jealousy and envy that everyone experiences and suggests ways to deal with them.

It is possible to be envious about many different things. You might envy someone because of his or her talent in a particular sport or music. You might envy a person who has lots of expensive possessions, such as designer clothes or the latest cell phone and MP3 player. Similarly, you could envy someone who is regarded as the best student in the class or who gets the lead part in all the school plays.

Envy is a normal emotion. Like all emotions, it can motivate you to do something. Envy can make you want to fight or work harder for something that you believe you want or need. However, envy is often described as a negative emotion, because when it occurs, you tend to feel badly about yourself. When you are envious, you see yourself as not having the talent or things that someone else has. In fact, you're likely to resent the person who inspired this bad feeling in the first place.

Feelings of envy may be fleeting or they may last over a long period of time, as it happened with Katie. Her envy created feelings of rivalry, or competition, with

You and Your Emotions

A part of everyone's personality, emotions are a powerful driving force in life. They are hard to define and understand. But what is known is that emotions—which include anger, fear, love, joy, jealousy, and hate—are a normal part of the human system. They are responses to situations and events that trigger bodily changes, motivating you to take some kind of action.

Some studies show that the brain relies more on emotions than on intellect in learning and in making decisions. Being able to identify and understand the emotions in yourself and in others can help you in your relationships with family, friends, and others throughout your life.

Ashley. This rivalry was one-sided, however. Ashley did not see herself directly competing with Katie any more than she saw herself competing with any other girl in their class. It was Katie who had come to feel that every test was determining which of them was smarter.

Jealousy occurs when you worry about losing an important person to someone else. Everyone gets jealous at one time or another. In fact, normal jealousy is just that—normal. But it causes unpleasant feelings. You're anxious and uncomfortable, overwhelmed by a range of emotions that often include fear, sadness, anger,

Jealousy: The Green-Eyed Monster

Have you ever heard the expression, "She's been bitten by the green-eyed monster" or wondered why people say someone is "green" with envy? Seventeenth-century playwright William Shakespeare has been responsible for many expressions that have found their way into popular speech, including this reference linking jealousy with the color green.

In Shakespeare's play *Othello*, the character Iago is envious of the success of his general, Othello, who has been recently promoted. To cause the man's downfall, Iago suggests that Othello's wife, Desdemona, has been unfaithful to him. Iago encourages Othello's jealousy, although at one point in the story he likens jealousy to a cat playing with a mouse before killing it:

> O, beware, my lord, of jealousy;
> It is the green-eyed monster which doth mock
> The meat it feeds on.

> **What's the difference?** Jealousy involves wanting to keep something which you already have; envy involves wanting something that you don't have.

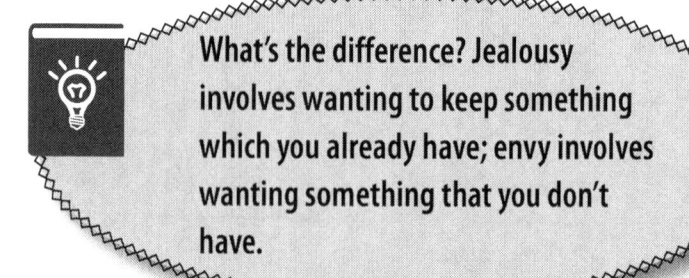

and shame. Jealousy typically involves uncertainty over relationships that are important to you.

It's easy to recognize the pangs of jealousy—they cause a strong, physical reaction: a sick sensation in your stomach may accompany the feelings of the fear of a loss. A tightened jaw and tenseness in the back and shoulder muscles may result from the feelings of anger over the belief that someone else is trying to "take your place" in your relationship. These physical responses to

> "The jealous are troublesome to others but a torment to themselves."
> —William Penn

"Envy asks one leading question: What about me? Why does he or she have beauty, talent, wealth, power, the world's love, and other gifts, or at any rate a larger share of them than I? Why not me?"
—Joseph Epstein

jealousy are your body's signal that something is "not right" or is lacking in your life. Because jealousy is a negative emotion, when you are jealous, you don't feel very good about what's going on.

Of the two emotions—jealousy and envy—jealousy is the more intensely felt emotion and the harder one to hide. If you are jealous of someone, you might deny it to him or her—and even to yourself. You might admit instead that you are angry with that person for some particular offense but stop short of recognizing that your own jealous feelings are actually making matters worse.

When people don't cope in healthy ways with feelings of jealousy and envy, they can destroy relationships and even act violently. However, jealousy and envy don't have to be destructive emotions. When properly handled, these feelings can have positive results. For instance, your envy of someone else's possessions can help motivate you to work hard to obtain those things you want. Similarly, engaging in a rivalry with someone can also be positive when it results in both rivals pushing harder to be the best they can be.

Although jealous feelings can make you feel badly about yourself, they can be helpful if you realize they are a signal that a relationship is important to you. Once you learn to recognize that signal—that you are feeling jealous of someone—and you understand why, you can take steps to react in a positive way. For instance, if you fear losing the respect and love of someone important

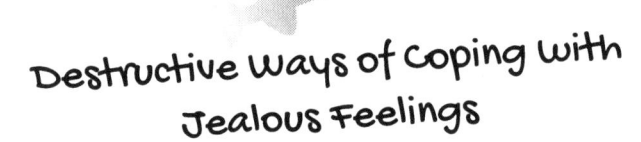

Destructive Ways of Coping with Jealous Feelings

- Demanding commitment
- Putting down or insulting a rival
- Denying that jealousy exists
- Avoiding or giving the silent treatment

to you, you can make sure to show the person you fear losing that you care about him or her. The following chapters can help you learn how to better understand your feelings of jealousy and envy. This book also includes tips on how to handle these feelings in yourself and in others.

CHAPTER TWO

How You Feel About Yourself

> *Alexandra was looking forward to going to the movies with her best friend, Rita, over the weekend. But on Wednesday, when Alexandra mentioned seeing the film together, Rita said that she wouldn't be able to go. She had been invited to a party at Kaisha's house that night. Alexandra felt an awful lurch in her stomach when she heard the news. Was her best friend abandoning her? she wondered.*

Feeling uncertain about where you stand in friendships—and other relationships—can be upsetting. And it can be hard to know when those uncertain feelings really have any basis. Just because Rita was busy on the night that Alexandra wanted to go to the movies, Alexandra believed her friend didn't want to have anything to do with her anymore. Part of what was making her uncertain were her own feelings about herself.

How you feel about yourself can have a big effect on your relationships with others. If your self-esteem—your own feelings of self worth—are low, you tend to be insecure in your relationships. And you get jealous more often than people who like themselves and believe in their own worth.

During the teen years, many girls are dealing with feelings of low self-esteem, and it can be tough. It is a time when you are going through puberty—the physical changes that occur as your body is maturing physically into that of an adult. In addition to feeling unsettled by the changes occurring with puberty, many girls are struggling with the image they have of themselves. They may feel unhappy about their weight, their looks, their complexion, their popularity, or their talents. (By the

---

Science Says...

The media has a strong influence on how you feel about your body, no matter your age, height, or weight. In a 2007 study at the University of Missouri-Columbia, researchers found that women in the study were negatively affected after viewing pictures of models in magazine ads for just three minutes. In all cases, the women who viewed the models featured in magazines such as *Seventeen* and *Glamour* reported feeling less happy about their own bodies when compared to another group that did not view the ads.

Physical and Emotional Effects of Jealousy

Some Physical Reactions of Jealousy
- Insomnia
- Rapid heartbeat
- Dizziness
- Nervousness
- Lack of appetite
- Sweaty hands
- Shakiness

Some Emotional Responses to Jealousy
- Sadness
- Fear and anxiety
- Shame and humiliation
- Anger and rage
- Feelings of helplessness
- Feelings of pain
- Hurt feelings

way, guys are struggling with many of these things, too.) At the same time, they may be finding that school is getting harder, and that relationships with parents and friends are sometimes strained or stressful.

Low self-esteem and aggression. Researchers have found that low self-esteem can cause problems in kids' relationships with one another. In a study published by Penn State University, investigators tried to determine what kind of incidents made kids upset or jealous in their friendships. The researchers used a Friendship Jealousy Questionnaire to evaluate almost 500 fifth-through ninth-graders. Students were also asked to rate their peers in terms of how jealous they were.

In the study, girls were found to experience more jealousy of their friends than boys. Researchers explained that because girls spend more time thinking about their friendships than boys do, girls may have higher expectations of how their friends should treat them. Researchers also found that girls who had low self-esteem were more likely to experience jealousy within their friendships, often mistaking ordinary behavior that friends exhibit as reasons for feeling betrayed and disrespected.

Furthermore, girls with a reputation among non-friends for being jealous were also considered to be aggressive. That is, they were more likely to engage in physical aggression, such as hitting or pushing. Or they engaged in relational aggression, such as isolating or ignoring a peer with whom they were angry.

High self-esteem. When you feel good about who you are and what you have, you are less likely to envy or feel jealous of other people. Similarly, you are more likely to support your friends in their successes and have them support you in yours.

CHAPTER THREE

Are You an Envious or Jealous Person?

Although it is normal to feel envious or get jealous from time to time, you may have concerns about your own feelings and behavior. There are various ways you can evaluate your tendency toward feeling envious or jealous. These methods can also help you determine if you are dealing with these feelings in a positive way, or if you might improve your behavior.

Evaluate your tendency toward envy. Are you happy when good things happen to others or do you resent their good fortune? How you answer the following questions will give you an idea of whether your feelings of envy could use some toning down. For each of the following situations, choose A or B.

1. You and your best friend both tried out for the soccer team. She made it.
   A. You congratulate her and say you look forward to attending her games.
   B. You say, "So I guess the coach knows your parents and didn't want to upset them by cutting you from the team."

2. A good friend announces her family is going to Florida and she is allowed to take one friend along. After you learn that she picked another friend from your group,
   A. You smile and tell her to have a good time.
   B. You point out that the weather is pretty lousy this time of year and you wouldn't have wanted to go anyway.

3. Your cousin who is the same age as you and goes to a different school is elected president of the National Junior Honor Society. When your parents pass along the news,
   A. You say, "That's nice; I'm happy for her. I'll congratulate her the next time I see her."
   B. You tell your parents that if you went to such an easy school, you'd not only be president of the honor society but also first in your class.

4. Your girlfriend comes over to show off her new cell phone—the one you've been dying to own. She shows all the features to you, including the ring tone she selected.
   A. You hold the phone in your hand, imagine what it would be like to own it, and give it back.

B. You go to your parents and complain that it is really unfair that they didn't buy the same phone for your birthday.

5. One of your guy friends asks if you know anything about Sue, a pretty girl who is new to the school.
   A. You offer to introduce him to her because she's in your math class.
   B. You wonder what he sees in her that he doesn't see in you and why he's never asked you out.

6. You are the lead singer in a small band and are approached by a girl with a great voice. She'd like to join your group.
   A. You say you'll talk to your bandmates about letting her in because you always vote on everything.
   B. You tell her that she's not right for the group.

Give yourself one point for every A answer and two points for every B. If you got six to eight points, you

"Jealousy is the tie that binds, and binds, and binds."
—Helen Rowland

are nearly envy-free. Anything above that indicates you could be having some issues with envy. Your behavior could be pushing your friends away if you don't put it in check.

Keep a record. Monitor yourself to see if you are having envious feelings or jealous thoughts more often than you would like. Start keeping a journal in which you list any situation or event that sets off feelings of envy or jealousy.

In your diary, distinguish between feelings of envy and feelings of jealousy. (Remember, you envy someone for what they have and you want. You feel jealous when you fear losing something you already have.) Make separate sections for each emotion. In the jealousy section, make four columns. Entitle the first column "Jealousy Triggers." This column will contain the situations that set off feelings of jealousy for you.

You typically envy people whom you admire—for having the ability or the wealth that you want for yourself. Instead of spending your energy obsessing over what others have, try to focus on what *you* have.

Then next to each trigger, make a note of how you felt when the situation occurred. In the third column, write a brief note explaining what you did or how you reacted (if you did anything). Make a similar section in your diary listing when you felt envious—of your friends, siblings, or others.

Analyze your journal. Take a look at your envy triggers and jealousy triggers and how you felt. As you look over each situation, ask yourself whether you had a good reason for your jealous thoughts. Or were you feeling jealous without any basis? Were you blowing a situation out of proportion or did you know that you had good cause for your feelings of jealousy? Answer these questions in notes that you write in the fourth column.

If you wrote that you felt threatened by something, try to figure out why you felt that way. When you identify what is making you jealous, you can get a handle on whether or not you have a reason to feel jealous. This journal can help you begin to understand your emotional reactions to envy and jealousy.

Only you can determine whether it is time to change your behavior or the way you relate to friends, classmates, boyfriends, and family members. But recognize that your envy and jealousy have the potential to have a negative effect on your relationships. Try to understand and use these emotions to take positive steps in improving how you relate to the people in your life.

Decide what to do with your jealousy. Most people feel anger when they are jealous, so it is important to get a handle on any angry feelings that may accompany your jealousy. In this case, the same techniques for managing anger apply for managing jealousy: if you find yourself stewing into a rage, try to take control of your heated emotions. Take several deep breaths and try to calm down. Look at the situation and try to identify whether you have a good reason to feel jealous. If you can, get another person's point of view. Perhaps other people don't think there is any reason for you to feel jealous—or perhaps they agree that there is a problem that needs fixing.

However, the best way to deal with your jealous feelings is to talk about them with the person whose behavior has upset you. If you think your boyfriend is flirting with another girl, let him know you are upset. But don't talk to him if you're in the middle of a jealous rage. If you recognize you're feeling overwhelmed by angry feelings, walk away from the situation until you can calm down.

When you are ready to talk about the situation, keep your cool. State your point of view calmly and quietly. Don't accuse or place blame. One way to express yourself when in a conflict is by using I-messages. These are statements that explain your point of view without making accusations or causing the other person to feel defensive.

Don't rage and vent. Try to explain why you are having jealous feelings. Ask for support from the other person—your friend, sibling, or boyfriend—in understanding why you shouldn't be jealous. Just as in resolving a conflict, try to reach a solution that allows you both to feel better.

CHAPTER FOUR

Sibling Rivalry

> Barbara has a younger sister who is pretty, popular, and smart—a straight-A student who never seems to need to crack a book. Barbara, who is two years older, also gets good grades, but she has to work a lot harder. She wishes everything would come to her as easily as it does for Marilyn.
>
> Barbara admits that she's jealous of her younger sister, but says she has good reason. Their parents always agree to whatever Marilyn wants—allowing her to stay out later than Barbara could when she was the same age. And they also always seem to take Marilyn's side whenever she and Barbara get into an argument. And lately, the two sisters have been having a lot of arguments.

Barbara's problem with her sister is a common one called sibling rivalry. If you have a brother or sister, you too may have found yourself bickering and arguing over a variety of issues. In fact, you often might not recall what started the argument in the first place. Many times the issue stems from feelings of competition, inadequacy, and frustration with one another.

Jealousy and envy can play a big part in sibling rivalry. A brother may feel envious of the accomplishments of his sister if she is getting straight As and is the top scorer on the school basketball team. Or an older sister can resent her younger sister for having the same curfew time of midnight, even though the older sister had to be home by 10 P.M. when she was the same age. Feelings of jealousy can also emerge when siblings compete in academics, sports, or the arts.

A major cause of sibling rivalry is jealousy over parents' attention. If you are the first-born, sibling rivalry can begin when your parents rock your world by bringing home a new baby. Suddenly you are forced to share the love, time, and attention that your parents can give with someone else. But anywhere you fall in birth order in your family can influence family dynamics.

> "Jealousy is all the fun you think they had."
> —Anonymous

> ⚛⚛⚛ **Science Says...** ⚛⚛⚛
> A 2006 story on siblings published in *Time* magazine reported a study by family sociologist Katherine Conger in which she concluded that many parents have a favorite child. After interviewing 384 pairs of siblings and their parents and studying their relationships over a three-year period, Conger concluded that 65 percent of mothers and 70 percent of fathers showed a clear preference for one of their children—in most cases, the older one.
> However, the same story reported the results of a June 2006 *Time* telephone poll that showed more than a thousand participants disagreed with Conger's conclusions. The *Time* poll indicated that just 18 percent of people said that their parents had favored one child over another in their families.

You may live in a family in which the eldest is always in charge of the other kids or the youngest receives special treatment.

Rivalries and bad feelings can worsen when kids think a parent likes one child better than another. Feelings of jealousy can escalate into angry conflicts involving arguing, name-calling, teasing, and tattling—as well as pushing, shoving, and hitting. If you recognize that you have an unhealthy rivalry going on between you and your siblings, there are steps you can take to make things better:

Talk it out. When you have a disagreement with your brother or sister, use words to try to reach an agreement or at least come to an understanding. It is important to try to understand the other person's point of view. Even if you end up deciding that neither one of you is going to budge from your position, at least you can agree to disagree. Learn to value the other person's perspective.

Figure it out. Do your best to figure out a solution to the problems that seem to come up again and again. Perhaps you are always arguing about who controls the

Built-in Competition

A little sibling rivalry can give you and your sibling the push you both need to excel in sports and academics. Tennis star sisters Venus and Serena Williams have used their sibling rivalry to set the world of tennis on fire. Just fifteen months apart in age, the two young women spend a lot of time together both on and off the court. However, when competing across the net from each other, they both play hard to win. The two superstar players deal with conflicting emotions. In 2002, when Venus lost to her younger sister at Wimbledon, she said, "I want to win, but I want her to win also."

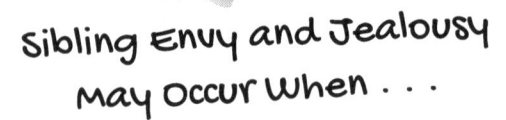

> ### Sibling Envy and Jealousy May Occur When . . .
> - A sibling has a talent that you don't have or is more like your parents than you are.
> - Parents make direct comparisons between their kids or make one kid feel like they like another sibling better.
> - Older kids think parents go easy on or spoil the younger ones or younger kids think they get less recognition than the older ones do.

television remote or who gets to sit in the front seat of the car. One way to avoid conflict over such issues is to keep track of who got the remote or had the honor of sitting in the front seat last. Be willing to compromise, negotiate, and take turns.

Bring in the big guns. If you and your sibling can't seem to settle the conflict between yourselves, you may need the help of a third party. Talk to an adult whom you trust. A parent, teacher, or school counselor might be able to give you another point of view or solution to your particular problem.

Go your own way. If you find that you are disagreeing with your sibling a lot, you might want to create some space between you. Take a break from hanging out together by spending some time alone or more time with friends.

Focus on your successes. You can feel bad about yourself if you're always thinking about the areas where your sibling's got you beat. Perhaps your sister is a better athlete or your brother always wins every video game you play with him. Don't dwell on your sibling's accomplishments. Instead think about the things that you do well. Direct your thoughts to the things you like about yourself.

Let your parents know when you think they're being unfair. If you believe your parents are treating your sibling better than they treat you, or if you feel like you are being unfairly compared to him or her all the time, let your folks know. In most cases, they are probably unaware of what they are doing. Once they know how

When a sibling teases, you can ignore the taunts, make a joke, tell him or her to stop, or ask for outside help.

you feel, they'll probably try to change. Meanwhile, don't blame your brother or sister for your parents' behavior.

Keep working at it. Treat your sibling the same way that you would like to be treated. If you want his or her respect, you have to be willing to show respect, too.

CHAPTER FIVE

Feeling Jealous of Friends

> *There were only four roles for girls in the school's musical play this year, but Savannah was sure she would get the leading role. After all, she had the best voice in the chorus—she was the only one who had a solo during the winter concert. But when Savannah checked the play director's final cuts posted on the bulletin board, she was shocked. Her best friend Madison had the lead, and Savannah's name wasn't even on the list.*

Just about everyone recalls a time when they have felt envious or jealous of friends. Even though you know you are supposed to be happy when something good happens to your friends, the reality is that sometimes you find it difficult to be happy for them. You can't help thinking that the same thing should have happened to you. Maybe your friend gets named editor of the school newspaper—which is a job you wanted—or makes the varsity tennis team and you end up on junior varsity.

Outside school, you might envy your friends for other reasons. Perhaps they have parents who let them

Feeling Envy and Jealousy Over . . .

Academics and school clubs. Your friend gets much better grades than you do or was just elected to the position you wanted.

Relationships. Your best friend starts hanging out with the new girl in town and you're not included. Or your friend may have a new boyfriend or girlfriend and now spends less time with you. Or even worse, your friend is dating the person you have a crush on.

Ownership. Classmates may have more expensive possessions—clothes, gadgets, money—that you would like to have.

stay out later than you. Or their parents buy them things you'd like to have. You may feel jealous of a friend who goes out on lots of dates, while you sit home alone.

When you feel envious or jealous of friends. The guilt and distress that often accompany the envy and jealousy directed toward friends can be stressful. After all, you are feeling overwhelmed with bad thoughts about people you like.

If you want to put a stop to such feelings, take charge of your thoughts. Instead of shooting lightning bolts of anger toward the person who won the role, took the job, or earned the award you wanted, change your focus from thinking about your envy. Recognize that your feelings may be based on a false assumption. For example, Savannah shouldn't leap to the conclusion that she wasn't chosen for the school musical because the director didn't think she was talented. Her friend may have been chosen simply because the director thought she had the right look for the particular role, not because she was the better singer.

Step back and think of something positive about yourself. Don't put yourself down. Avoid negative thoughts by focusing on good things about yourself and what the future can bring. For example, Savannah could remind herself that she was good enough to solo at her school concert, and that there would likely be other opportunities for her at next spring's music concert.

Envy in Consumer Culture

Everywhere you go, advertisers are trying to get you and your friends to buy something. Visit the Internet, and pop-up ads vie for your attention. Go to the movies and there are coming attractions inviting you to see yet another movie. Turn on the TV, and you will be bombarded with ads for cell phones, clothing, MP3 players, and other things that the commercials declare you absolutely must have in order to be happy. Sometimes you'll be able to get these things, but sometimes you won't. Your friend might be the one with the newest must-have item . . . and you might find yourself envying that person for her good fortune.

You can fight that envy and save yourself some money by asking yourself the following questions about the advertised product:

- Is this something I truly need?

- If I got it, would I wear it or use it a lot or quickly get tired of it?

- Could I borrow it?

- How much would it change my life if I got it?

- Would I be willing to sell something else to get it?

- If I had to work for it, how long would it take me to save up for it?

- Would it be worth it?

Best Friends Forever—or Not

- Recognize that as maturing people discover new interests, they want to meet new friends.

- If your friend is hanging out with someone new, you might want to try to make friends with the new person, too.

- Give the situation time, and your friend will most likely seek you out after the novelty of the new friendship wears off.

- If a best friendship ends, understand that it's not necessarily the new person's fault or anyone else's. Sometimes people just grow apart.

Get motivated. If you're envious of a friend who can afford all the latest fashions, rechannel your feeling of envy to one of motivation. If owning the same designer jeans would make you happy, put your energy into thinking about what you could do so you could buy them. You could ask to be paid for doing extra chores around the house or for other people. Or you could find a part-time job and earn the money you need.

However, be aware that being able to buy the newest fashions or latest technologies of today's consumer society won't necessarily ease your feelings of envy. You may find that having the cash to buy whatever you want is not necessarily going to bring happiness. In fact, before you buy, take some time to think whether you really want the item. After you give it some thought, you may decide that having the same things as everybody else is really not necessary for you.

When friendships feel threatened. You may find yourself experiencing feelings of jealousy because your best friend is spending more and more time with the new girl at school. If a good friend has started hanging around with other people—and doesn't seem to have as much time to spend with you these days—it can hurt. Feeling jealous is normal. But spending all your energy brooding over your feelings won't change anything.

There are some things you can change—simply by making the effort. You can try talking with your friend to find out why she's spending less time with you. You can let her know you miss spending time with her. And you can try to get to know the new girl, too, so that you both can hang out with your best friend.

However, if it looks like your good friend isn't interested in keeping your friendship, think about adding some new friends to your own circle. You might try joining a new club at school or participate in a local youth group. Get to know new people by going out of your way to talk to people in your class you don't know well. Remember, you can make choices about what to do with your jealousy.

When others are jealous of you. Let's say you've done something amazing and you expect that your best friend will be really happy for you, but she isn't. Her lack of enthusiasm may not bother you the first time it happens. However, if her response is negative every time something good happens to you, you will want to do something about it.

When Others Are Jealous of You

Don't automatically assume someone is "just jealous" if they don't seem to like you.

Be proud of your accomplishments, but recognize you don't need to talk about them a lot; bragging can make others feel bad and make you seem conceited.

Recognize that gloating doesn't make anyone feel good.

Acknowledge that it is possible for you to be competitive and proud of yourself, without tearing others down.

Realize that people who are jealous might be rude to you without any cause; their bad behavior is not your fault.

If you think your friend is feeling jealous because you've done something that she wishes she had done, you can be a good friend by pointing out some of her positive accomplishments. Help her feel better about herself by talking to her and sharing some of the things about her that have impressed you most. Remind her of her past successes, and how happy you were for her at those times. On the other hand, if she has expressed her jealousy by saying the occasional mean thing to you or about you, do something about it. Rather than allowing a nasty remark to slide by, ask her directly, "What do you mean by that?" Let her know that her remarks are insulting and that she is hurting your feelings.

Before getting angry about other people's jealous behavior, you might also want to look at your own behavior. Are you bragging a little too much about your good fortune? People get pretty tired of a person who gloats and appears self-involved. You might want to tone your own actions down a bit.

If you have figured out the cause of your friend's envy or jealousy, you might benefit by talking about the issue in gentle terms. For example, if your girlfriend pouts whenever you bring up your boyfriend because she isn't going out with anybody, you might say something like, "Would you like to double date with one of Mike's friends and me?" or "Who do you think is cute in history class? Let's figure out what you can do so he'll talk to you."

Sometimes, no amount of empathizing (understanding and sharing of feelings) or talking to your friend will get her over her envy—at least not right away. If it appears that she won't change her negative thinking, you might have to spend less time with that person. You might even come to the conclusion that the friendship cannot be saved.

CHAPTER SIX

Jealousy in Dating

Anna and Jake have been dating for two months. Anna likes Jake but has noticed that he talks to a lot of other girls. She sometimes wonders if he likes her as much as she likes him. She finds that more and more often she is worrying that another girl will soon take him away from her.

Like friendships, dating relationships can be affected by jealousy and envy. Understanding another person's needs when starting in a dating relationship can be hard. In Anna's case, she is struggling with feelings of jealousy and is not sure if such feelings are normal. And she's not sure what she should do about it. Feelings of jealousy are normal, especially when the other person behaves in a way that is confusing to the person he claims to care about.

Feelings of jealousy aren't necessarily bad for a relationship. A little bit can be healthy, if it causes

Tips on Dealing with Romantic Jealousy

- Recognize that when dating someone, you need to spend time with other people, too.

- Keep in mind that healthy relationships—and friendships—require trust.

- If your crush or ex is going out with someone else, it's normal to feel a bit jealous—but realize that there's probably not much that can be done to change the situation.

- You may feel better by talking to a good friend or a trusted adult about your feelings. Or you might want to take your mind off of your jealous feelings by focusing your energy and time on something else, such as volunteering or learning something new.

the people involved to pay more attention to their relationship and work at improving it. The best way to sort out problems in a dating relationship between two people is to be honest with each other. For instance, if Anna thinks Jake is flirting with too many girls, she needs to address the situation with him. It won't help for her to dwell on how mad she is at him or how to get back at the girls he's talking with.

Jealous feelings can affect not only the two people in a dating relationship but also their friends. Just the fact that a girl is dating someone when her friends aren't can cause problems within her friendships. According to one survey about dating, conducted by *USA Weekend*, the majority of teenagers admit to being jealous when their friends start dating before they do.

When either you or your friends are dating, there will be some changes in your relationship with each other. In order to spend time with your boyfriend you will probably be spending less time with your girlfriends. That can lead to hurt feelings as your girlfriends might feel left out and unimportant to you. Meanwhile, you feel like you're in the middle of a tug-of-war between the people you care about.

Making the dating relationship work. Getting to know someone besides your friends and family is new territory to explore. It is a "learn-as-you-go" process. As you learn more about this new person in your life, you'll want to keep in mind the hallmarks of a good relationship by thinking about these questions:

Does he like the real me? When you date, you want to be "real" with your guy and not put on a show based on what you think he'd want you to be. You should feel comfortable enough to be yourself. And you should

Dating Basics

Maintain your interests. You were a separate person before you met your boyfriend and should continue to have outside interests after you're a couple.

Your boyfriend does not have the power to make you feel bad about yourself or to feel like a loser—unless you give him that power.

Communicate openly and honestly. Make it a habit to tell your boyfriend how you feel and encourage him to be open with you.

Be aware that your earliest dating relationships may not last long because you and your boyfriends are still learning about what you are like as people.

---

have a sense that he recognizes some of your best traits, like your upbeat personality and zany sense of humor.

You also need to see and accept your boyfriend as he is and respect him for his unique qualities. For instance, you might appreciate that he always looks out for his little brother. Or you might like the fact that he is honest enough to tell you when he is uncomfortable in certain situations.

Jealousy in Dating

Does he trust me? If your guy gets upset when you just talk to another guy, he may have a jealousy problem. There is nothing wrong with a little jealousy, but he shouldn't overreact to an innocent situation. If you can't reassure him that all is well, then he's likely to feel that way again—and that behavior isn't healthy in a good relationship.

Does his opinion count more than mine? Going out with someone provides the opportunity for you to make lots of choices. What movie do you want to see? Which party do you want to go to? What do you want to do tonight? In a good relationship, both members make decisions. When there are disagreements about what to do, both people are willing to make compromises. One person does not get his or her way all the time.

Am I losing my identity? Dating someone should not mean that you sacrifice your friendships and interests to make the relationship work. You want to continue being the person that you are. You should continue to meet new people and do the things you always enjoyed with the friends you had before you met your guy. And you want to allow him to do the same thing.

What would you do if the guy you liked asked you to spend all your time with him to the exclusion of your friends? The first thing to do is ask him why he is requesting that you put him before your friends or give them up altogether. Maybe he doesn't think they like him or he doesn't feel comfortable around them. By talking about the issue, you may think of a way to smooth things over or understand his position.

However, you may come to realize that the reason he has made this demand is because he is possessive or controlling. He may be asking you to choose between him and your friends because he believes you should be seeing only him. No one in a healthy dating relationship should make demands in which you must give up your friendships. You need to think hard about whether you'd be better off with him or without him.

Do we communicate with each other? If something is bothering you, will you come out and tell him, or will you keep your thoughts to yourself? Can you expect him to share what is on his mind, too? It is important to talk with each other and to understand where both of you are coming from. If you don't ask questions, you might resort to guessing what your boyfriend means and you could be wrong.

In any relationship, communication is important. If you are unhappy about something, you need to share it. However, it is important to talk about your problems in a way that doesn't place the blame on your boyfriend. Instead of saying, "You shouldn't have done that," say "I felt awful when you did that."

When you use sentences that start with "I" instead of "you," you are letting your boyfriend know how you

Using I-Messages

Express your feelings in a non-threatening way by using I-messages. An I-message typically has four parts:

1. How you feel ("I felt jealous...")

2. The action or incident that bothers you ("...when you flirted with Shannon...")

3. Why you feel the way you do about what happened ("...because I know she likes you.")

4. How you'd like the situation to be resolved ("Next time you see her, would you make it clear that you already have a girlfriend?")

feel. "I-messages" are solution-oriented statements that use the word "I," rather than "you." Because I-messages describe only the way that you feel about a situation, the person listening to them is less likely to feel defensive. I-messages don't blame or judge the person you're having a problem with. They allow you to let that person know there is a problem in a way that does not make him feel uncomfortable.

CHAPTER SEVEN

Irrational Jealousy

> Mia was worried about her friend Brittany. Whenever Mia invited her friend out to a movie, to go shopping, or to go anywhere, Brittany would always say that she had to call her boyfriend Todd first. "I'm just making sure it was okay with him," Brittany would say. She explained that Todd loved her so much, he would get mad if he didn't know where she was. Lots of times, though, Todd would tell Brittany she couldn't go out with Mia because he wanted to see her. Over vacation break, Mia hadn't seen her friend at all. Yesterday at school, Mia finally met up with Brittany, but she didn't have time to talk. Mia thought she looked nervous and unhappy.

Jealousy is not the same thing as love. Yet in many cases, a girl may believe that because her boyfriend acts jealous that he really cares for her. In reality, jealousy is the fear and anger about the possibility of losing love. (It can also include other emotions such as sorrow and shame.) Extreme jealousy and possessiveness in relationships can destroy them.

While most people tend to get over jealousy after a short time, some people continue to obsess. They are uncomfortable when the person they love has contact with anybody else. People who demonstrate this extreme form of jealousy, also known as irrational jealousy, typically make unreasonable and unfair demands on a person in a relationship. Uncertain about the strength of their relationship, they take offense at their loved one's contact with others—regardless of whether there really is any threat.

For example, suppose a girl found a note in her boyfriend's backpack with another girl's phone number on it. She could ignore it, thinking there was a perfectly logical reason the note was there. Perhaps the guy had

Recognizing Jealousy Warning Signs

1. Blames you or others for his problems and feelings
2. Needs to know where you are all the time
3. Acts possessive of you
4. Doesn't have any friends except for you
5. Calls you offensive names
6. Threatens you
7. Hits you or breaks things when angry

Adapted from "Teen Dating Violence," October 2004, Washington State Office of the Attorney General

the number because he's working on a science project with the girl at school. However, someone with irrational jealousy would immediately jump to the conclusion that the phone number was there because he was interested in another girl. She'd be furious.

People with irrational jealousy remain obsessed with finding proof that their suspicions and fears are true. After their jealousy triggers have been aroused, such people stay jealous for long periods of time. They tend to have difficulty in controlling their anger and become abusive toward the very person they claim to love.

Because they are insecure, extremely jealous people tend to expect the worst of other people. They may be clingy, needy, demanding, and resort to threats or tears to get their way. Unable to understand any viewpoint except their own, people with irrational jealousy can also be controlling and obsessive, expecting the loved one to always abide by his or her wishes. A boyfriend may try to control all aspects of his girlfriend's life—wanting to know where she is at all times, telling her what to wear, what friends she can see, and how to behave. A jealous girl may behave in a similar way with her boyfriend, becoming angry or giving him the silent treatment when he spends time with his friends or says something nice about another person. Such relationships are abusive.

The Survey Says...

In 2006, Liz Claiborne Inc. commissioned a survey of more than 1,000 American teenagers, ages thirteen to eighteen, to determine their experiences with abusive and controlling relationships. The Teen Relationship Abuse Survey revealed that extreme jealousy among teens is a very serious problem that needs to be resolved:

64 percent of teens in serious dating relationships were dating someone who "acted really jealous and asked where they were all of the time."

25 percent of girls said it was OK for guys to be really jealous.

21 percent of those in relationships had dated someone who tried to stop them from seeing their family or friends.

20 percent of those who had been in a serious relationship said they had been hit, slapped, or pushed by their boyfriend or girlfriend.

Experts agree that teens who have not had much experience dating may not recognize the warning signs of an abusive relationship. Sometimes young people mistake jealousy, possessiveness, and pressure to have sex as signs of love. Rather than try to get out of an abusive situation, they will remain, not understanding why the "love of their life" is making them so miserable.

Many teenage girls find it hard to tell their parents or friends when a relationship has turned abusive. That's because the parents' first reaction is typically to forbid their daughter from seeing the guy again. That's not the result the girl is looking for; she wants to make things good again, like they were in the beginning of the relationship. Similarly, she may not tell her friends because she thinks it is her fault that there are problems in the relationship.

Abusive relationships may not be obvious at first. Evidence of abuse may only show itself a little bit at a time. If you are new to dating and unsure about what is acceptable dating behavior and what is not, you might not recognize a bad situation at first. Take a look at the jealousy warning signs on page 50.

If you (or a friend) are involved in a relationship with someone who exhibits these signs, you should talk to an

According to the Centers for Disease Control and Prevention, up to 12 percent of teens nationwide are estimated to be in a physically violent dating situation. Experts say that the best thing to do if a teen feels he or she is in an abusive relationship is to get help—tell a trusted adult or contact a domestic violence group.

Safety Tips for Getting Out of an Abusive Relationship

People with irrational jealousy may try to prevent their loved one from breaking up with them by threatening to kill themselves. They may also threaten to physically harm the person trying to leave. When in a rage, an abusive boyfriend may hurt his girlfriend by slapping, pushing, shaking, or shoving her. Here are some tips to help end an abusive relationship:

Tell him it's over. If you fear for your safety, you don't have to tell him in person that you want to break up. However, if you must meet face-to-face, make sure you are in a public place.

Don't have contact with the person again. If he tells you he will harm himself if you do not see him, let a trusted adult know what he has said. He needs help, but you need to remain safe.

Keep your friends close. Take a friend with you when you attend dances and other social activities. If you walk home from school, have someone walk with you.

Plan ahead for possible emergencies. If you have a cell phone, keep it with you so you can get help in an emergency. If one is not available to you, carry a phone card or enough change to use a pay phone. Decide on a special code word that will signal your family that you feel in danger. (If you find yourself in a potentially dangerous situation and are unable to say so, you can use the code word to let them know.) Remember that you can phone 911 if you are afraid.

Ask for help. Talk to your parents to let them know what is going on and listen to their suggestions. They may choose to contact the other person's parents, or even the police, to let them know there's a problem. You shouldn't be dealing with this kind of situation on your own.

adult you trust about what to do. To ensure your safety from someone who might actually present a danger to you, you need to get outside help. Get in touch with your school or community counselor, or contact your religious leader. You may want to call the number for the domestic violence hotline or the dating abuse helpline, which features Web-based information as well as a telephone hotline, listed on page 63.

Counseling can help both the person who exhibits irrational jealousy and the victim of domestic abuse. Professional counseling by a social worker, psychologist, or other mental health professional can help someone with irrational jealousy learn how to recognize and control harmful behavior. Such therapy can also help the victim of abuse to develop better self-esteem and recognize that irrational jealousy is not normal behavior in any relationship.

CHAPTER EIGHT

Overcoming Your Green-Eyed Monster

Maybe you think that your feelings of jealousy and envy are hurting the relationships you have with your family and friends. If so, be aware that you can fix things. It's possible to keep the green-eyed monster from taking over your life. Some of the following suggestions can help put you on the right track:

Learn to recognize what makes you jealous. Identify your jealousy triggers (for example, maybe you have an uneasy feeling when you see your boyfriend talking to his ex or when he doesn't answer his cell phone). Think about why these situations make you feel jealous. If seeing him talking to his ex makes you feel jealous, you can recognize that you are uncertain about your relationship. If you don't feel comfortable because he is not answering his phone, you might have a problem with trusting him. Knowing what triggers your jealousy can help you learn more about yourself and what is important to you.

Admit to your feelings. Don't try to suppress your jealousy—use it. Try to view that flush of jealousy or twinge of envy as a positive thing. Once you realize these emotions are signaling that something is not right with how you feel about your relationships or yourself, you can choose a healthy way to respond.

If you are jealous of your boyfriend's friends because he hangs out with them and plays video games, use your jealousy as a signal that you would like some changes in how he is treating you. You need to communicate better with each other so that he considers your wishes, too. Don't whine and complain. Share your feelings in a positive, non-threatening way. But be sure to talk about what is bothering you!

> "Normal" jealousy can provide the spark to respond to a threat. It increases a person's alertness, stimulating him or her to take action.

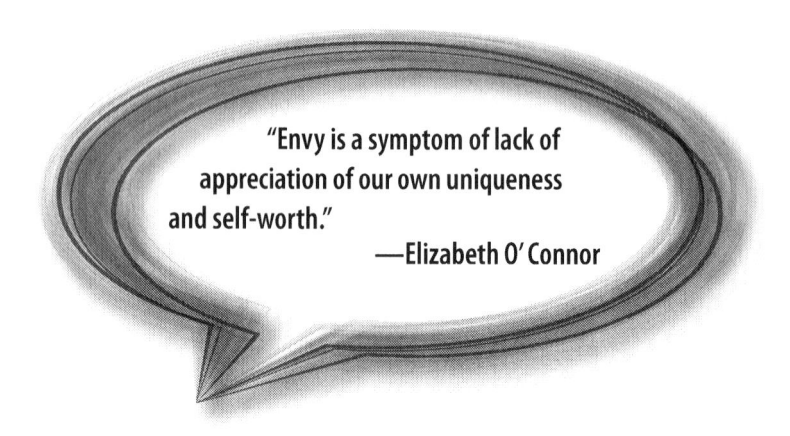

"Envy is a symptom of lack of appreciation of our own uniqueness and self-worth."
—Elizabeth O'Connor

Use your feelings to motivate yourself. Use your jealousy to motivate yourself to work at improving the relationship. Normal jealousy—in small doses—can let the other person know you care. Instead of taking his or her attention or affection for granted, you are sensitive about how to maintain your relationship.

Use your envy to make some changes in yourself. Think about what actions you can take that will help you achieve what you want. If you envy a classmate's good grades, use that feeling to change your behavior. Study a little harder or improve your study habits.

Remember, it is okay to be envious of someone else once in a while. "Looking at the other girls around you and wondering what you can learn from them is perfectly normal," says Cheryl Dellasega, author of the book *Surviving Ophelia*. "If you don't, you may be

Things to Do When You're Being Dragged Down by Jealous Feelings

Ride your bike, roller skate, run, or dance to music. Physical activity of any kind can instantly lift your spirits and make you feel good. That's because during physical activity the body releases mood-boosting chemicals called endorphins.

Learn something new. Join a new club at school or take a course outside school like yoga, meditation, or kickboxing. Any new skill you pick up will make you feel better about yourself.

Help other people. Volunteer as part of your school's community service project or at the local hospital or animal shelter. Help your mom with the dishes without being asked or assist your sister with her homework. Or simply say something nice to someone else who looks depressed. Being there for other people can help you see how important you are.

Adapted from "The Story on Self-Esteem," Kidshealth.org

missing opportunities to develop yourself." When you take positive action because of your envy, that's a good thing.

Focus on your positive qualities. Remember, a lot of people feel jealous, insecure, inadequate, or vulnerable at one time or another. Since envy and jealousy often result from a lack of confidence in yourself, you can avoid these emotions by building up your own self-esteem.

Don't let your envy focus on what you're doing wrong or on the areas in which you lack talent. Give yourself a break from negative thoughts about your hair, your weight, or the lousy grade you just got on your English test. Instead, take stock of your good qualities. Make a list of the good stuff you can do and have done: your smile, your top score on the last math test, or your singing voice. Maybe you are organized, always on time, or good at sudoku and other math puzzles. Or you can run the mile faster than anyone in your gym class. Make the list of your positive traits as long as possible. Be sure to add some items that you wish you were good at and ways you plan to try to get better at those that you aren't good at.

Keep it in perspective. The things that you really want to have today—and that influence your feelings of envy—are most likely to change over time. Consider this: is what you think you can't live without now going

Boost Your Self-Esteem

Write down what you do best. Create a list of big and small stuff that you do well. Think about what other people compliment you about and what you yourself know to be true.

Tell yourself three good things every day. Look for evidence of things you did well that day.

Appreciate yourself. Instead of focusing on whatever shortcomings you think you have, tell yourself about your body's good points: the dimples that emerge when you smile, the little nose you share with your mom, the red highlights in your hair, and the hands that work so well at playing the piano.

Ignore the negative voice you are hearing in your head. Don't think about what you aren't, what you haven't done, or don't have. When you start putting yourself down, recognize what you are doing and give it a rest. Instead, channel positive messages about yourself—for example, about how your mom appreciates that you look after your little sister or that your friends know they can depend on you to listen and help them with problems.

<small>Adapted from "Building Self-Esteem: A Self-Help Guide," Substance Abuse and Mental Health Services Administration's National Mental Health Information Center</small>

to be as important to you a year from now? By putting your needs in perspective, you can more easily decide how much energy you want to put into obtaining each item on your "want to have" list.

Remember, you can choose how you cope with your own feelings of envy and jealousy. Don't let them control you. Instead, use them as signals that something in your life needs to be changed. However, if it seems like your jealousy or envious feelings are becoming a problem in your life or if you're having trouble working through them, seek outside help. Talk over your feelings with a good friend, a trusted adult, or your school counselor, and consider their perspective and advice.

FIND OUT MORE

Books

Becker-Phelps, Leslie. *Insecure in Love: How Anxious Attachment Can Make You Feel Jealous, Needy, and Worried and What You Can Do About It.* Oakland, Calif.: New Harbinger Publications, 2014.

Espejo, Roman. *Frequently Asked Questions About Jealousy.* New York: Rosen Publishing Group, 2007

Internet Addresses

loveisrespect.org (National Dating Abuse Helpline)
http://www.loveisrespect.org

Nemours Foundation TeensHealth: Am I in a Healthy Relationship?
http://kidshealth.org/teen/your_mind/relationships/healthy_relationship.html

Hotlines

National Domestic Violence Hotline
1-800-799-SAFE (7233)

National Dating Abuse Helpline
1-866-331-9474

INDEX

A
abuse, 51–55
aggression, 17–18
anger, 16, 24, 51

B
birth order, 27–28
body image, 15

C
communication, 24–25, 40, 45, 47–48
compromise, 46
consumer culture, 36

D
dating, 42–48

E
emotions, 7, 8, 10, 11, 12, 16, 22, 23–24, 29, 49, 51, 57, 60
envy
  and the consumer culture, 36
  coping with, 22–25, 35, 37–38, 56–62
  definition of, 6–8

F
families, 26–32, 53, 54
friendships, 14, 17–18, 33–41

G
"green-eyed monster," 9

H
hotlines, 55

I
I-messages, 24–25, 47–48
irrational jealousy, 49–55

J
jealousy
  coping with, 22–25, 35–41, 56–62
  and dating, 42–48
  definition of, 6–7, 8–10
  emotional reaction to, 16
  and friendships, 14–15, 17–18, 33–41
  physical reaction to, 10–11, 16
  and self-esteem, 14–18
  triggers, 22, 23, 51, 56–57
  unhealthy ways of coping with, 12
journals, 22–24

M
motivation, 7, 8, 12–13, 37, 58

O
Othello (Shakespeare), 9

P
parents, 27–28, 53, 54
possessions, 34, 36
puberty, 15

Q
quiz, 19–22

R
relationships, 14–15, 17–18, 34, 49–55
rivalry, 7–8

S
self-esteem, 14–15, 17–18
sibling rivalry, 26–32
surveys/studies
  friendship and jealousy, 17–18
  irrational jealousy, 52
  jealousy and dating, 44
  parents' favoritism, 28
  self-esteem, 15

T
triggers, 8, 22, 23, 51, 56–57

V
violence, 11–12, 53, 55

W
Williams, Serena, 29
Williams, Venus, 29